110 TIPS TIME·SAVERS & TRICKS OF THE TRADE

110 TIPS TIME·SAVERS & TRICKS OF THE TRADE

Edited by Wayne Rice

Compiled by The 1984 National Resource Seminar For Youth Workers Team:
Mike Yaconelli, Tic Long, Jim Burns, Rich Van Pelt, Dave Hicks, Denny Bellesi, Bill McNabb, Steven Mabry, Mike Giarrita and Wayne Rice

Cover Design: Jerry Jamison
Graphic Design: Gary Bell
Illustration: Tim Pagaard

A Youth Specialties Book

**110 TIPS, TIME SAVERS, AND TRICKS OF THE TRADE
FOR YOUTH WORKERS**

Copyright © 1984 by Youth Specialties, Inc.
1224 Greenfield Drive
El Cajon, CA 92021
(619) 440-2333

ISBN 0-910125-04-X

INTRODUCTION

AT first glance, this book may appear to be
. . . well . . . small.

But looks can be deceiving!

Take a CLOSER look.

Hmmm . . .

As a matter of fact, this IS a small book.

Let's look at it another way.

A famous person once said, "You forget
most of what you read anyway!"

So, by reading this book, you have *less to
forget.* (There's some incredible logic there
somewhere.)

Actually, this book contains a lot that you'll
want to remember.

The 110 "words of wisdom" in this book
were compiled by a group of youth workers
with a combined total of more than 130 years
of youth ministry experience.

We asked them to come up with an even
100 key tips that every youth worker should
know.

We settled on the 110 that you find here.

(*You* try picking the ten to leave out.)

Even though this book is small, we hope
you'll take it seriously.

Give each item some thought. Don't just

race over the material, but put some creative thinking into each one.

Take the principles and extrapolate a few ideas of your own.

One other thing.

Don't think you have to do everything in this book.

These tips were not meant to be a job description for the perfect youth worker.

On the other hand, don't be afraid to try them out.

They just may work for you.

We think that these tips will benefit you greatly.

Use them with our best wishes.

Youth Specialties

ONE

ALWAYS take pictures of your youth group activities. Hang them up on the church or youth group bulletin board. Have kids create crazy captions for them.

TWO

SUBSCRIBE to a popular magazine like *Rolling Stone* or *Teen* that will help keep you on top of the current youth culture.

THREE

USE the mail a lot. Send birthday cards and personal, affirming notes to each of your young people. Send postcards and announcements on a regular basis.

FOUR

USE surveys and questionnaires to their best advantage. Find out what your young people are thinking on a regular basis.

FIVE

JOIN a youth workers' fellowship in your area. If none exists, organize one. Meet periodically with other youth workers in your area to share ideas and problems. They can be a great resource for you.

SIX

DON'T meet in a room that is too big for your youth group. If your group is small, meet in a small-sized room. This gives kids the feeling of being "packed" in. Always make sure your meeting place is casual and comfortable.

SEVEN

AVOID making promises to parents you can't keep.

EIGHT

GET an automatic telephone answering device for your youth group. Have the phone company install a separate line, and use that number as an information center or "hot line." People can call anytime and get details for upcoming events and activities. Parents especially will love this.

NINE

GIVE kids the opportunity to reflect on what they have learned after each meeting. Have them write down "I learned . . . ," or discuss what they have learned in small groups.

TEN

NEVER ignore a disturbance during a meeting. When a distraction occurs, acknowledge it. It's the best way to regain the attention of the group.

ELEVEN

HAVE the young people in your group put together a "youth group yearbook" at the end of the year. It should include photos and articles about the past year's activities. It will be a positive reminder of the good times shared by the group.

TWELVE

PREPARE a good job description for yourself and stick to it.

THIRTEEN

IF your group is small, go in with other groups on things. Pool your resources. Share costs. Don't be afraid to invite another youth group to some of your activities, even if they are of another denomination.

FOURTEEN

ALWAYS deal with problems as they come up. Don't expect them to go away on their own. They won't.

FIFTEEN

S ET up a "phone chain" to help spread the word regarding upcoming events. If you have ten young people who will call ten other kids, you can personally contact a hundred kids in one evening. Personal contact is always the most effective.

SIXTEEN

IF your church does not have a good youth resource library, then start one. It should grow every month. Include books for kids, their parents, and your leaders.

SEVENTEEN

ALLOW the young people in your group to select adults in the church whom they would like to have as youth sponsors. It's easier to enlist those adults when they know they have been chosen by the kids.

EIGHTEEN

VOLUNTEER to be a
sponsor or chaperone for
events and activities at your local
junior high or high school. Most
schools need help for the
lunchroom, dances, assemblies,
field trips, or sports events.

NINETEEN

MEET regularly with your
volunteer staff and
sponsors for training, prayer and
fellowship.

TWENTY

PERIODICALLY keep track of your time for a week to see where it is *really* going.

TWENTY-ONE

ALWAYS arrive at the church or meeting place early enough to greet youth and their parents as they arrive. Stay late for the same reason.

TWENTY-TWO

DEVELOP programs that reflect the needs, interests and energy level of the young people in your group, not the adults who work with them.

TWENTY-THREE

TAKE two days away from the office to prepare for busy times during the year.

TWENTY-FOUR

HOST local high school international students at a dinner in their honor. Have them tell about being a teenager in their country and how that differs from the United States. Present each one with a gift certificate for a free call home from your youth group.

TWENTY-FIVE

PLAN some early morning or late night activities. There will be few conflicts and the kids will enjoy the adventure.

TWENTY-SIX

DEVELOP realistic goals and expectations. Don't depend on immediate results to determine success or failure. The harvest is at the end of the age, not at the end of your meeting. Real results come later. Often much later.

TWENTY-SEVEN

TAKE a local youth worker (from another church or para-church organization) to lunch. Don't talk about kids.

TWENTY-EIGHT

WHEN planning activities for your youth group, consider the late afternoon from 3:00 p.m. to 5:30 p.m. Many young people have nothing to do during this time and are left unsupervised because of working parents.

TWENTY-NINE

PREVIEW everything. Never use a film you haven't seen or book a speaker you haven't heard. Your young people should not be treated like guinea pigs.

THIRTY

GET to know the parents of your young people. Learn their first names and use them.

THIRTY-ONE

TAKE time to read several new books each year. Try to read a book on youth ministry, a book on time management, a book on theology, one of the "classics," and a couple of popular novels.

THIRTY-TWO

FIND positive ways for your young people to become involved in the life of the church—not just the youth group. Get them serving on boards and committees, working with children or the elderly, participating in worship, and attending other events and meetings. Avoid creating a "youth ghetto."

THIRTY-THREE

DON'T be afraid to smile and laugh a lot.

THIRTY-FOUR

VISIT each of your young people at their homes. Ask to see their room. Note how it is decorated and what they have on display. This will give you good insight into your young people.

THIRTY-FIVE

PRINT up a brochure or postcard that describes your youth group and its activities. Include photos, brief descriptions, times and locations (if known) and make these brochures available to parents, youth group members and new young people who might be unfamiliar with the group.

THIRTY-SIX

PLAN at least two retreats a year. One day at a retreat is worth a month of Sundays.

THIRTY-SEVEN

LET kids be kids. Don't expect them to act like adults. If you do, they will always disappoint you.

THIRTY-EIGHT

NEVER cancel a meeting or event simply because not enough kids showed up. You may need to adapt or change plans, but don't send everybody home. Let those who show up know that they are just as important as those who don't.

THIRTY-NINE

LISTEN to the music that your young people listen to once in a while. Weekly radio programs like "American Top 40" will help you stay current. Discuss the music in a positive way with your kids on a periodic basis.

FORTY

TAKE a Red Cross first aid course. Encourage others on your youth staff to do the same.

FORTY-ONE

KEEP a "referral file" for crisis counseling. If you feel inadequate or unsure of yourself, don't hesitate to refer young people to professionals who have the appropriate training and experience.

FORTY-TWO

OFFER to serve as a volunteer chaplain at a local hospital adolescent unit or drug/alcohol treatment program.

FORTY-THREE

GET a set of Ideas books from Youth Specialties. You'll never be able to use all those ideas, but next time you need one, you'll have plenty to choose from.

FORTY-FOUR

ESTABLISH a "skit closet" full of costumes, old clothes, and props that you can use for skits and plays. Ask people in the church to donate ridiculous looking clothing and other items. Great stuff can be found at a local thrift shop.

FORTY-FIVE

COMMUNICATE availability. Don't give young people the impression that you are too busy for them.

FORTY-SIX

WHEN students help you with a game in front of the group, don't make fun of them. Use crowd breakers and stunts to build up students. Make heroes out of them, not idiots.

FORTY-SEVEN

HAVE a hobby or some outside interest. Learn to play a musical instrument, start a collection of something, or take up a new sport.

FORTY-EIGHT

DON'T do everything yourself, even though you can do it better. Learn to delegate.

30

FORTY-NINE

ALWAYS have at least one youth program "in the can" for emergency use. It will come in handy when your guest speaker doesn't show up or your film doesn't arrive.

FIFTY

ASK adults in the church to "adopt an adolescent" by getting to know one of the young people in your group and praying for him or her on a regular basis.

FIFTY-ONE

IF your favorite songs are not in a songbook, put the words on overhead transparencies or on slides. If the songs are copyrighted, get permission first.

FIFTY-TWO

DON'T neglect the "nerds" of your group. Give them as much of your time and attention as the sharp kids.

FIFTY-THREE

INVITE the senior pastor to attend a youth group activity occasionally to give him exposure to the kids and the program. This also gives kids a chance to see the pastor as a real person.

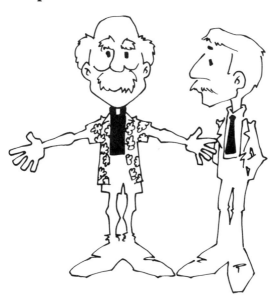

FIFTY-FOUR

TEACH your leaders by your own example to be like player-coaches in ministry.

FIFTY-FIVE

KEEP parents informed. Publish a parents' newsletter or schedule periodic meetings for parents where they can ask questions and provide input. Lack of communication with parents can seriously handicap your ministry.

FIFTY-SIX

USE older couples as adult sponsors. Give students role models who have been married longer and have experienced more.

FIFTY-SEVEN

GET a Resource Directory from Youth Specialties. It's like a "yellow pages" for youth ministry. It will save you hours when you want to find the best resource for any situation.

FIFTY-EIGHT

SET a goal for each activity and see if you meet it. This will give you direction for everything you do.

FIFTY-NINE

DEVELOP good job descriptions for your volunteer leaders. Make sure they know exactly what is expected of them as well as what is *not* expected of them. Provide them with good resources for the job that you have asked them to do.

SIXTY

TRY to "catch" your co-workers doing something right. Give them a hug and compliment them for doing so well.

SIXTY-ONE

MAKE sure every meeting and activity is well organized. It lets young people know they are important, and it reduces discipline problems.

SIXTY-TWO

CONDUCT brainstorming sessions with your young people to foster creativity. Allow ideas to flow without criticism. Evaluate only after the ideas have stopped.

SIXTY-THREE

NEVER use religious jargon and worn-out cliches. Say what you mean in words that young people can understand.

SIXTY-FOUR

SAY something positive to each of your young people. Compliment them when they are alone, or in groups, or in front of others. This helps build self-esteem.

SIXTY-FIVE

WHEN your students have obvious flaws, like complexion, stuttering, weight, or personality, never assume that they are already being helped.

SIXTY-SIX

WHEN talking to young people, use personal illustrations to keep the message alive. Abstract ideas need concrete examples.

SIXTY-SEVEN

NEVER use curriculum without first adapting it to the needs of your group. Curriculum writers don't know your kids; you do.

SIXTY-EIGHT

HAVE a place to keep clip art, brochures, cartoons, drawings, illustrations, and lettering that you find from time to time. This can be used later for designing your own publications and announcements.

SIXTY-NINE

DON'T worry about numerical growth. Size does not equal success. Health leads to growth; not vice versa.

SEVENTY

HAVE a personal bulletin board in your office where you post pictures of your friends, young people in the group, classic postcards and other junk that you collect. Kids love to look at it and it gives them a glimpse into your personality.

SEVENTY-ONE

DON'T take yourself or your circumstances too seriously. Nothing is ever as bad as you think it is, and nothing is ever as good as you think it is.

SEVENTY-TWO

BE able to say "I don't know." Young people will then listen to you better when you do know.

SEVENTY-THREE

ALWAYS re-confirm any group reservations or bus charters the day before the event.

SEVENTY-FOUR

AVOID all double standard rules for staff counselors and students. Whatever goes for the kids should also go for you and your staff.

SEVENTY-FIVE

DEAL with root causes, not symptoms in your teaching. Rather than fighting or preaching on behavior, find out what is the cause of the behavior and deal with that.

SEVENTY-SIX

ATTEND the National Youth Workers Convention, or a National Resource Seminar for Youth Workers, or some other training event on youth ministry once a year. Never think you've learned it all.

SEVENTY-SEVEN

DON'T make threats that you can't or won't follow through on.

SEVENTY-EIGHT

KEEP a supply of games and recreational items in the trunk of your car at all times. You never can tell when you will need a football, a Frisbee, or a few water balloons.

SEVENTY-NINE

MAKE sure you have at least one male and one female adult youth sponsor working with your youth group.

EIGHTY

ALWAYS serve refreshments at meetings and activities. It's a relatively easy thing to do and young people love it. It also keeps them around a little longer for personal contact.

EIGHTY-ONE

TAKE advantage of the free films and videotapes that are available from your local public library.

EIGHTY-TWO

DON'T worry about the problem of cliques. Instead, provide plenty of opportunities for everyone to interact with each other and to discover each other. Breaking up cliques is usually an exercise in futility and somewhat counter-productive.

EIGHTY-THREE

KEEP a file on each of your young people. Get family and personal information, vital statistics, photos, notes from personal interviews and observations, and other information. Keep it confidential. Not only will it benefit your ministry, but it will make a wonderful gift for your successor.

EIGHTY-FOUR

WHEN trying it improve the church, start with yourself.

EIGHTY-FIVE

AVOID counseling someone of the opposite sex in a private place. If you must counsel a person of the opposite sex, prevent rumors and unfortunate misunderstandings by meeting in a public place, like at a coffee shop or at the park.

EIGHTY-SIX

KEEP a youth ministry journal. Each week, record and evaluate what you did with the youth group. Describe contacts with kids and reflect on each one. This will help you to organize your thoughts and to remember important events.

EIGHTY-SEVEN

HAVE a group of adults who you can go to for advice or counsel. You need the accountability and support that this will provide.

EIGHTY-EIGHT

NEVER reveal a confidence that a young person or a parent entrusts to you. No matter how well intentioned you may be, doing so will almost always have disastrous results. There are exceptions, such as a life-threatening situation, but exceptions are rare.

EIGHTY-NINE

TAKE your student leaders on a retreat to plan and to become a team.

NINETY

VIDEOTAPE the "big game" this year at your local high school and show it after the game on a wide-screen T.V. Invite the whole school.

NINETY-ONE

DON'T force yourself into the lives of kids where you might not be welcome.

NINETY-TWO

IF you have young people who play guitars, allow them to play for group singing. This will not only build their confidence and leadership ability, but possibly improve your singing.

NINETY-THREE

VISIT the schools where your young people attend. If possible, introduce yourself to the principal, the teachers, and the coaches. Let them know who you are.

NINETY-FOUR

MAKE learning the names of kids a top priority. You'll never have a ministry to them until you know and remember their names.

NINETY-FIVE

AVOID disciplining young people in front of their peers. It's best to handle discipline problems privately on a one-to-one basis.

NINETY-SIX

KEEP a spare projector lamp handy for the next time you show a film or slides.

NINETY-SEVEN

LEARN the art of spontaneity. Call some kids and invite them to go to the beach with you the next day, or on a hike, or to a movie. "Kidnap" a few kids and have a big slumber party at your house. Do something unpredictable now and then.

NINETY-EIGHT

NEVER believe camp and conference center brochures. Always visit a facility before booking it. Ask questions about flexibility, additional costs and availability of "extras." Eat a meal if possible.

NINETY-NINE

WHEN leading a discussion, refrain from making overly positive or negative comments when young people offer their opinions. Remain as neutral as possible. This will encourage openness and honesty.

ONE HUNDRED

LEARN to say "no." Keep time for your family, your outside interests, and your personal growth.

ONE HUNDRED ONE

MEET on occasion in the homes of church board members so that they can see first-hand what the youth group is like.

ONE HUNDRED TWO

USE television to your advantage. Tape and discuss good programs. Discuss and evaluate the programs that are most popular with your young people.

ONE HUNDRED THREE

HAVE your youth group provide coffee and donuts, a salad bar, or some other refreshment after the worship service, either as a gift to the church or as a fund raiser.

ONE HUNDRED FOUR

GET a good re-fillable calendar that will enable you to plan your youth group activities at least a year in advance. If you don't know where you're going, you probably won't get there.

ONE HUNDRED FIVE

BECOME a listener. Learn to withhold your opinion on everything and just listen. You will be much more helpful that way.

ONE HUNDRED SIX

GET your group involved in at least one service project each year. Service projects not only give kids a chance to make a positive contribution to someone else's life, but they are great for building community.

ONE HUNDRED SEVEN

PUT on a drama once a year. This gives more kids a chance to use their talent and be in the limelight.

ONE HUNDRED EIGHT

BEGIN a ministry at a local youth detention center. Involve students if possible. Offer to help the chaplain with counseling or chapel services.

ONE HUNDRED NINE

DON'T be afraid to be a model for your young people. Whenever you can, take a student with you. Let them be a witness to your life as you do the common, everyday things— shopping, fixing the car, being a parent. Let them see you as a real person.

ONE HUNDRED TEN

DON'T attempt to be "one of the kids." If you are an adult, be an adult. Just be an adult who loves kids.